Korean-American Experience
in the United States

Korean-American Experience in the United States

Initial Thoughts

Christian Kim

The Hermit Kingdom Press
Cheltenham ♦ Seoul ♦ Bangalore ♦ Cebu

**Korean-American Experience in the United States:
Initial Thoughts**

Copyright © 2004 by Christian Kim

All rights reserved. No part of this book may be reproduced in any form or by any means, electronic or mechanical, including photocopying, recording, or by any information storage and retrieval system, without permission in writing from the publisher.

ISBN 1-59689-008-8 (hardcover)
ISBN 1-59689-009-6 (paperback)

Library of Congress Control Number: 2004116476

Write-To Address:

The Hermit Kingdom Press
3741 Walnut Street, Suite 407
Philadelphia, PA 19104
United States of America

Info@TheHermitKingdomPress.com

★ ★ ★ ★

Hermit Kingdom
12 South Bridge, Suite 370
Edinburgh, EH1 1DD
Scotland

http://www.TheHermitKingdomPress.com

Dedicated to Koreans in America

"All that I am, or will be, I have learned from my family, my friends, my teachers, and training with the sword."

King Sejong the Great
Jo-Sun Dynasty of Korea
(May 6, 1397 - May 18, 1450)

CONTENTS

Preface [13]

The Korean-American Church [17]

Economic Struggles of the Parents [37]

Social Struggles of the Parents [51]

Korean Youth in America [67]

The Great Korean Tragedy [87]

Preface

There are over a million Korean-Americans living in every corner of the United States of America. Some have distinguished leadership positions; others contribute to the society through manual labor and other service jobs. Most Korean-Americans are very happy to be in America, particularly in the process to make the country better for everyone, including themselves.

Each and every Korean-American has individual experiences that are unique. And certainly, Yale University Law School Dean Harold Koh's experience is not the same as the experience of Mr. Jae-Choon Shin, an immigrant from Brazil who started a clothing store in Southern California from scratch and expanded it into a multi-million-dollar clothing company. And the story of my father, Rev. Manwoo A. Kim, who has served as a senior pastor of a Korean-American church in Philadelphia for decades is not the same as the experience of my sister's Korean-American friend at Calvin College who was adopted by a Dutch-American family at the age of one, whose family relations are almost primarily Dutch.

But in the midst of all the differences and the diversity, there are remarkably shared experiences that can be called, "Korean-American." Either by active involvement or by tangential social relations, Korean-Americans of different backgrounds and experiences have participated in a type of Korean-American experience. Unfortunately, not enough has been written on the subject.

This book is an effort to turn things around. Of course, I recognize that one book will be constrained by space and thematic limitations. And I do hope I will write more books on the subject in the future to fill in the gaps. For now, I am happy to share some initial thoughts on the Korean-American experience. I believe that this book will give you a good picture of the greatest commonality in the Korean-American experience.

I hope that your life will be enriched by learning about a community that is becoming more and more significant in American social, political, economic, religious, and civic life.

Christian Kim
Korean Independence Day, 2004
Jesus College
Cambridge
United Kingdom

Korean-American Experience in the United States

Initial Thoughts

THE KOREAN-AMERICAN CHURCH

Korean-American Experience in the United States

In the spring of 2003, I attended KASCON (Korean American Student Conference) conference at Cornell University and represented Cambridge University Korean Society (CUKS). I felt it my duty to the Koreans in Cambridge to represent them since I was the president of CUKS for the 2002-2003 academic year. And I am glad that I was able to do that. Not only did I enjoy rubbing shoulders with other student leaders of Korean descent, I learned quite a lot from the conference.

There were many impressive things at the conference, and many speakers and showcases highlighted the achievement of Koreans in the western context. The first female Asian-American judge in Maryland spoke about her experience of growing up with a Korean face and working in places where she was the only Asian. She talked about implicit institutional racism that is implicitly approved without critical thinking. There was a reporter for 20/20 who shared her experiences at Stanford University as a student active in Asian-American movements. Unlike Stanford, where fully 1/3 of all the students are Asian, she found a different reality in the TV business. She shared the joys and sorrows of her struggles for recognition as a qualified Korean-American.

My friend from Cambridge University, Rev. Dr. Paul Lim, who recently became a professor at Gordon-Conwell Theological Seminary spoke on the Korean-American Christian experience. In the process, he shared quite a bit about his personal struggles as a Korean-American trying to wade through institutional and social barriers during his long journey that included an Ivy League education and doctoral studies at Cambridge University in the United Kingdom.

What became quickly clear is that whatever the field which these leaders worked in, they had to fight through social and institutional obstacles. However, they found many friends along the way who were supportive and helpful. There were individuals concerned about human rights and equity, who went out of their way to lend a helping hand and to deflect attacks from intolerant individuals who were bent on impeding their progress.

In the American context, it certainly did not hurt that there are many evangelical Christians who fundamentally support equality. This is clear in the appointments by President George W. Bush, a Fundamentalist Christian who does not even drink alcohol. President Bush appointed the first African-American US Secretary of State in the person of Colin Powell. President Bush appointed the first African-American National Security Advisor in the person of Dr. Condoleezza Rice. And President Bush also

Korean-American Experience in the United States

has a long-standing record of promoting Hispanic-Americans and Asian-Americans to very high government posts.

There are many ethics-minded evangelical Christians like President George W. Bush who are willing to see beyond color and promote excellence regardless of religion. Korean-Americans have benefited greatly from the presence of evangelical Christians in America. Countries that do not have many evangelical Christians tend to be less aggressive about fighting for the rights of the people of color and getting them actually appointed in leadership positions and acting as leaders.

And it has not hurt that many Korean-Americans tend to be active evangelical Christians, aggressively subscribing to the Fundamentalist dictim, such as the prohibition of pre-marital sex, drinking alcohol, and aggressive emphasis on Christian evangelism. Many Fundamentalist Christians in America actually see Korean-American Christians as a great ally. This is evident in the numerous religious leadership positions that Korean-Americans hold in America across Christian denominational lines.

KASCON, held at Cornell University, highlighted the impact of Christianity on Korean-Americans. And the importance of Christianity seems to be growing among Korean-Americans. When Rev. Dr. Paul

Lim asked the packed room who went to a Christian church during their high school days, everyone raised their hand.

Every single Korean in the room had gone to church as a high school student. We are talking about dozens of Korean college and graduate students from all over the United States and many different universities. Although I knew that most Koreans in the USA socialize around Korean-American churches, I was somewhat taken aback by the totality of the response.

Of course, 100 per cent of the Korean students in the USA do not go to a Christian church. Not all Koreans in the USA are associated with a Christian church. However, it is undeniable that the majority of Koreans have the Christian church as the primary social association outside of the family.

The Korean church has become not only a place of social association, but a center for cultural preservation. Most Korean schools are tied to a local Christian church. It is at the Christian church that many second generation Korean-Americans receive exposure to the Korean language, history, and culture. Often, the Korean church provides the strongest of friendships for even the second generation Koreans, and these Korean friendships help advance Korean culture in the community.

In short, the Korean-American church has become a reference point for new Korean immigrants as well as preceding generations of Koreans in the USA. The question is: How was this done? How is it that the Korean-American church came to play such a central role in the lives of almost all of the Korean immigrants, regardless of where in the United States?

In answering this question, I would identify several key factors: (1) Church's religious role, (2) Church's social role, (3) Church's cultural role, (4) Church's political role.

First, I will discuss the religious role of the Korean church in America. Most Korean churches in America have a clear sense of their religious mission. Whether they are Presbyterian, Baptist, Methodist, or Catholic, Korean Christians have taken an aggressively evangelistic outlook. Most Korean churches have proactive outreach programs to convert Koreans who are not Christians. At the center of proselytism efforts is the idea that salvation comes only to those who believe in Jesus Christ as God, Lord, and Savior. As almost all Korean churches hold to this tenet of the Christian faith, they are aggressive in wanting to share "Christ's love" with Koreans.

Most Korean immigrants to the USA tend to be Buddhists or non-religious so Korean churches had no dearth of people to convert. Korean Churches often engaged in "mass Christian outreach" programs in which they would visit various Korean families who recently arrived in the New Land and try to encourage them to attend the church. As many Korean church members are recent immigrants themselves, they have been able to relate to new immigrants in many ways. Common experiences often proved to be effective for recruiting new Korean immigrants to churches. Furthermore, the fact that Korean church members and new immigrants primarily spoke Korean provided an effective communication channel for relaying the Gospel message.

As new Korean immigrants quickly became absorbed into the Korean church system, they became recruiters of other new Korean immigrants. The system, which was not consciously thought out but developed naturally, became an effective means to proselytize most of the Korean population in the USA quickly.

The fact that Korean-American churches have very active programs solidified active Korean membership in the Christian church. Most Korean churches, regardless of denomination, have daily morning prayers. Most Korean churches have Wednesday and Friday prayer/Bible study meetings. And there are several worship services on Sundays. Active religious association has played an important role in cementing Korean religious communal identity.

Most Koreans attending Christian churches are clearly serious about their Christian faith. The religious enthusiasm of Korean-American churches gives their members a sense of mission that provides them with a meaning in life. As many Korean immigrants experience difficulties facing new immigrants, the Christian church gives them a sense of comfort and worth.

Generally, as Korean-American churches become more stable, they actively take on new responsibilities. For instance, many Korean churches sponsor evangelistic programs. Korean churches sponsor missionaries on a local and international levels. Many Korean churches (regardless of denomination), with senior pastors who can communicate in English, become involved in local Billy Graham Crusades.

I remember how active my father, a staunch Presbyterian, supported Billy Graham Crusades more enthusiastically than local Baptist ministers. When Rev. Billy Graham came to the Philadelphia area for evangelism, my father sponsored 40 nights of prayer for the church community and encouraged every church member to remember Rev. Billy Graham in prayer during daily family devotions. My father is representative of the aggressive support in the Korean-American community for Rev. Billy

Graham. My father along with other Philadelphia area leaders recruited volunteers from the Korean-American community to help out with the local Billy Graham Crusades.

Besides aggressive support of domestic Christian evangelism, every Korean-American church generally sponsors American missionaries in foreign lands. This is done normally along denominational lines. So, a Korean-American Presbyterian church would sponsor a white, black, or Hispanic Presbyterian missionary in a foreign country. And a Baptist Korean church will sponsor a Southern Baptist Convention missionary in Ghana.

Furthermore, all Korean-American churches sponsor Korean missionaries somewhere in the world. Most churches seek to produce missionaries to export to areas which are devoid of Christians. And often even church members get involved in this enthusiastic goal. For instance, there are many cases of successful Korean shop owners – deacons and elders in the church -- retiring early and going off to Vietnam or to Africa as missionaries until their dying days.

The religious role of the Korean-American church is perhaps the most significant and clearly the dominant factor of the Korean church experience in the United States. However, religious role is not the only role that the Korean church plays. The Korean church has a very important social role.

When Korean immigrants arrived in the USA, many of them could not communicate in English. They were completely unaware of what it meant to be in the USA. Korean culture is very different from American culture, and Korean laws are not the same as American ones. Korean immigrants really had nowhere to turn for help, except to the Korean church. There were no American social institutions and social work agencies which really met their needs. The Korean church filled in the gap.

Often, Korean pastors help new immigrants with everything from getting a driver's license to purchasing/renting the house and getting the first job in America. Korean pastors work over-time during weekdays to fill the needs of new immigrants. Without their help, many Korean immigrants would be totally lost. Many Koreans who have succeeded in America recognize the important social role that Korean-American churches have played in their most difficult times. Thus, it is not surprising that most Korean-Americans have the greatest of respects for the Christian church. Even those who did not convert to Christianity will recognize the important role of the Korean-American church.

Certainly, the positive social function of the Korean-American church is a contributing factor for why many Koreans converted to Christianity. Many Koreans saw in the sacrificial work of Korean churches and Korean pastors the love of Jesus Christ. Some initially stayed with the church out of a sense of gratitude even though they did not believe in Christianity. But attending the Christian church, many came to adopt and uphold the tenets of Christianity. The genuine Christian dedication of the converted immigrant community can be found in the extent to which many of them want to ensure that their children become "born again." Many Korean parents assiduously send their kids to summer Bible camps and Christian youth crusades.

Besides providing new immigrants with social services which they otherwise would not have, the Korean-American church provides social services with a Christian flavor for the established Korean-American community. Even many established Korean immigrants, often working 15 hours per day and not being familiar with the American society, depend on the Christian church to provide social programs for their children (and for them as well). And they welcome the Christian focus.

For many Korean immigrants, social programs that they enjoy the most in any given year are sponsored by the Christian church. Korean-American churches often sponsor trips to Niagara Falls or Washington,

DC. Since many Korean immigrants do not speak fluent English, the tours provided by the church are particularly welcome. Of course, there is praying and even a mini-worship service during the course of the church-sponsored trip.

Besides social recreation programs, the Korean-American church often provide a haven for the elderly. The grandpas and the grandmas who come over from Korea and feel completely disconnected from the new world around them find themselves in a community around the Christian church. Korean-American churches focus on providing programs geared toward the elderly and also provide information for attaining social benefits available to the elderly from the US government. Many Korean elderly would not have been able to collect their benefits if it weren't for the Korean-American church providing updated information and helping them to get the applications through.

The vital social role that the Korean-American church has played in the USA cemented its role as a place of central import for the Korean-American community. Especially, as Koreans in the USA experienced discrimination and other negative social repercussions, the Christian church became a symbol of social protection.

The Korean-American church was also able to crystallize its central role in the lives of Koreans in the USA by playing a very important cultural role. The Korean church generally is the primary preserver of Korean cultural practices in a Korean immigrant community. For instance, on New Year's Day, Korean immigrants often wear the Korean traditional clothing (Han-Bok), and there is a time when the young in the church show respect to the Korean elderly in a traditional manner.

Other Korean cultural festivals are often observed by the Korean-American church community. Certainly, any element that would conflict with Christianity is taken out, and all cultural celebrations are done with a Christian flavor. For instance, there is a prayer to the Triune God in thanksgiving, which is not an element in traditional celebrations.

This highlights the effective way in which the Korean-American churches have preserved the integrity of Korean cultural practices while Christianizing them. Most Koreans perceive the Christianized versions as just as Korean. The Christian reference point has become that central to Korean identity. It might not be surprising that Christianity and Korean cultural presservation go hand in hand given the past history.

During the Japanese Occupation of Korea (1910-1945), it was mostly the Korean Christians who fought to overthrow colonialist oppression. Many Korean Christians were killed as Korean patriots. Many more Korean Christians were killed as Christian martyrs as the occupying Japanese forces sought to enforce their world-vision in the occupied territories.

Most Korean Christians are proud of this chapter of Korean Christian history and celebrate it. Korean churches in America celebrate the proud heritage of Korean Christianity and its role in the preservation of Korean culture from the colonialist power. Thus, it is not surprising that almost all the Korean churches in the USA actively celebrate the Independence Day (August 15, 1945). It gave Korean Christians freedom to worship Christ without persecution and the opportunity to practice Korean culture.

The Korean church does not only celebrate corporate Korean culture but also foster opportunities to celebrate Korean culture as individuals. The best example is found in weddings. Often, after a Christian marriage ceremony, the newly married Korean couple follows the traditional practice of showing respect to the elders as a couple. Many married couples claim in hindsight that this was the most memorable part of the post-wedding ceremony and that it was gratifying on an individual level.

And certainly an obvious way in which Korean culture is well-preserved is via Korean meals. Korean Christians fellowship frequently around meals, and they are almost always very Korean in social form and content. Members of the Korean church often showcase regional specialties from back home. Often, Korean church fellowship meals are lavish and better than restaurant food. Food is a very important part of Korean culture, and the celebration of Korean food and the distinctive Korean emphasis of socializing around food are both preserved.

As many Korean churches take a type of house church meetings seriously, quite often smaller groups of church members will gather together in houses for meal fellowship and prayer. Food served in these meetings held in homes is almost invariably Korean food like the meal fellowships in churches.

And the Korean culture is also kept alive through Korean schools attached to Korean churches. Korean songs and stories are performed for the parents. Gospel stories are sometimes contextualized in Korean settings and performed as well. Korean churches often function as a place for creative expression and a place to explore Korean cultural concepts in light of the western context.

As Korean churches are so central to the Korean communal experience in the USA, it is not surprising that they play an important political role as well. In fact, for many Korean immigrants, the Korean church provides the best channel of connection to the outside non-Korean world. Political information is sometimes analyzed and discussed by Korean pastors. Invariably, they will be discussed in light of Christian standards. Often, political analyses resemble those of Dr. James Dobson or Dr. James Kennedy as Christian worldview is the most treasured in Korean churches.

In terms of political activism, Korean churches have not been as active as African-American churches. Perhaps, this is due less to the lack of interest in political issues than it is due to the lack of communication skills in English as most Koreans in Korean churches tend to be immigrants. The history of Korean immigration is relatively young in the USA. In terms of composition, most Koreans in the USA are first or second generation immigrants. Thus, political involvement has to be seen in light of their immigration experience and cultural shock in the west. It is certainly true, however, whatever political consciousness and activism that exist are effectively mediated through the Korean-American church.

Many Korean-Americans who are elected to a political office have a central support of the Korean churches. And their political connections have been formed through church connections. For instance, a Korean would enter the Democratic party successfully through the help and support of

African-American churches, which are in communion with Korean-American churches. And Koreans who are active in the Republican Party have the support of non-Korean Baptists and Presbyterians in many cases.

It is clear that it would be difficult to understand the Korean-American experience in the United States without understanding the role of Korean-American churches in the context of American culture and experience that support Christianity. Korean-Americans tend to be on the evangelical side of Christianity, and, thereby, have received unfettered support from American Fundamentalists and evangelicals when they needed help the most. Korean-Americans continue to safeguard a Christian vision for their communities in America.

And now, it is clearly evident that more and more Korean-Americans are becoming leaders of general American Christianity as well. For instance, a Korean-American held the highest leadership position of the biggest Presbyterian denomination in America with millions of members just a few years ago. Most American seminaries (of all Christian denominations) typically enjoy the presence of 20-50% Koreans in their student body. So, the trend will only continue and grow.

Given that with President Ronald Reagan, the Christian Right has been ushered back into the US government and American public and civic life, the evangelical character (of the American Fundamentalist Christian kind) of the Korean-American Christian community spells good things for the Korean-American community in the future even on a sociopolitical level.

The success of the Korean-American community which is becoming more and more public and visible came with great sacrifice. We have seen how the Korean-American church and Korean-American clergy have selflessly worked on behalf of the Korean-American community. Many American (non-Korean) evangelical Christians have lent a helping hand in times of need. But no mention of the Korean-American success would be complete without recognizing the tremendous sacrifice of Korean-American parents on behalf of their children who reap the benefits of their sacrifice. And it is now to the valiant struggles of Korean-American parents that I now turn.

Economic Struggles of the Parents

Korean-American Experience in the United States

If you ask Korean parents why they came to America, most of them will give the same answer: "For my children's education." And it would be difficult to say that this is not the case. Most Korean immigrants to the USA had a better life in Korea. This makes logical sense because immigration to the USA required a lot of money. Not only was money needed for the move, the American government accepted only "desirable immigrants" who could show that they could stand on their own two feet. The amount of money required for the move to America was particularly high in the post-Korean War Korea of 1960s and 1970s, before South Korea experienced the economic miracle and became one of the top-10 economies of the world.

Many Koreans left behind a bright future in Korea and sold their properties in order to immigrate to the USA. Majority of the Koreans who immigrated to the USA had at least a high school education, and many had finished college studies as well. They were leaving behind security of Korea for the promise of the American dream. In many cases, the dream was for their kids and not for themselves. Most of them were willing to tackle whatever difficulties that lay ahead in America.

The trend in Korean immigration is as follows. Koreans moved into poor, depresssed areas in the first instance. They were able to afford the cheap rent, and the money they brought with them could last longer in economically depressed neighborhoods. Often, these areas were not safe areas, so stories of Koreans being robbed were not uncommon. Some Korean children were mistreated by their peer group in rough neighborhoods.

For the first few months, Korean parents sought to find work. The kind of job Korean immigrants could land varied based on how much money they brought with them and what skills they had. More often than not, most Koreans did not have enough money to open their own business, and many did not have marketable skills to begin with in the new land. But Korean immigrants found a way to survive and eventually thrive.

There are several "types" of Korean immigrant business experiences. Often, a type is representative of thousands of Korean immigrants. And a commonality of experience can be perceived through the types that I will outline here.

(1) The "Sweat-shop" type: A Korean mother would go into a clothing factory and work at the sewing machine or other types of machinery for producing clothing. She would work 6 days a week for 8+ hours, while her husband works elsewhere. She would learn the clothing trade in the years that she spends there, save money

assiduously in the bank, and go prematurely grey. After working many years in this capacity, she would combine the money she and her husband have saved along with other capital they were able to raise or borrow and rent a cheap space.

There, they would open up a clothing factory and work 15 hours a day to get the business off the ground. In the process, the mother will use the knowledge and the connections she has acquired during her time in the clothing factory to make her shop a success. She makes quality clothing with interesting designs and minimizes cost of production. She sells the clothing at wholesale prices to retail stores, particularly utilizing her Korean connections. Distribution is generally to many small stores in the beginning.

Soon, she gains greater confidence as a wholesaler and lands major contracts from bigger department stores, generally focusing on providing quality clothing at inexpensive prices. She begins to see annual profits in the mid-6 figures. Both the husband and the wife are working hard together at the factory.

(2) The Mechanic type: A Korean father, who is a college graduate from a prestigious Korean university, comes to America. Finding that he cannot put his chemistry degree to use because of his problem with English, he finds that he has to find a totally new trade to support himself

and his family. He was always pretty good with his hands and had hobbies of building model planes and fixing his house, when he was in Korea. He decides that he will learn something that involves his hands. He knows enough English to take a technical course on being a mechanic.

After the six month intensive course, which he struggled through, while his college graduate wife worked as a waitress at a local Korean restaurant, he starts working in a local garage. The pay is bad but it allows him to practice what he has learned and find out the potential of the trade. After years of working, he and his wife put their money together to move into a row house that has garage space. It's still in a poor neighborhood, but this is a step up from the two bedroom apartment where his family of 5 has been living.

The father uses the garage to start his own business. He sends out flyers among the Koreans in the city, promising lower cost and faster service. As there are not many Korean mechanics in the city at the early stage of Korean immigration in the city, many Koreans bring their cars to him for minor repairs and routine check-ups such as oil change and tire change. They can't really speak English and feel comfortable talking to him in Korean about their car problems. He works 15 hours per day to keep up with rent payments and also to save money to open a proper garage. His hands are perpetually black from all the mechanical work. As there are not proper equipments for doing serious repair job on cars, it is not easy to make a lot of money from repairs. In the first instance, he engages in only minor repairs.

It takes him 6 years to save enough money to put a down-payment on a garage with proper equipment. He works 13 hours per day to keep up with house rent payments and garage payments. After working 3 years, 13 hours per day, 6 days a week, he begins to see a ray of sunshine. He begins to make good profit on top of his rent payments. He hires few extra mechanics right out of the institute that he graduated from, and his operation grows. He is able to finish the payment on the garage and puts a down-payment in a suburban home. 7 years from purchasing the garage, he is averaging $300,000 income per year.

(3) The Korean grocer type: A Korean couple arrives in the city. They are both college educated but they are the first from their families to go to college. They originated in a rural, farming community near Pusan, South Korea's second biggest city. They made an agreement to give their children the world and came to America with what money they were able to save up from their work.

Having grown up in a rural community, they are quite knowledgeable about fruit and vegetables. They are used to early hours and the farming community schedule. They understand that the secret to selling fruits and vegetables is freshness. They rent a one-room grocery store with a one-bedroom apartment attached to the second floor in a very rough neighborhood. They figure that this is their best chance for success. Neither of them feel confident about climbing up the ladder by working for others. They want to open a store on their own.

By talking with other fruit and vegetable store owners among Korean immigrants, they find out where they could get fresh vegetables and fruit. They both wake up at 4 AM to drive 1 hour and 30 minutes twice a week to get fresh vegetables for their store that opens at 8 AM. Their hard work in finding fresh vegetables and fruit pays off, and they attract customers from a wide area. Their fresh fruit and vegetables section encourages their custommers to purchase other grocery items in their store. Soon, they start making a good profit.

They put a down-payment on a house at a better neighborhood, and they plan for a family. They hire a recent Korean immigrant to work for the store as his wife is a few months pregnant. The husband takes full responsibility for the business and works together with hired help to improve the store. The husband lets his worker live upstairs for free. It helps the new immigrant, but it also helpsim, the owner, because the worker provides security for the rented store when the owner goes home after work.

After a couple of years of making profit, the owner has enough money to put a down-payment to purchase a store of his own. The owner finds a good deal in a neighborhood closer to his home and purchases it. It's bigger. He adds a fresh fish section and makes it a fresh fish market with fresh vegetables and fruit. He makes regular trips to pick up the fresh fish and two trips per week for the fresh fruit and vegetables. He is working 13 hours per day. He's working harder than ever but he is making a profit of $200,000-$400,000 per year.

These three "types" are only examples of the kind of routes that Korean immigrants have taken in the USA. There are other examples, of course. In all of these cases, there is a common underlying element. There are many hours of daily hard work. The Korean immigrant family works hard to save as much as they can. They take risks and put all that they have into their venture.

The good news is that most Koreans succeed. Some take 10 years, some take 20 years, but many Korean immigrants break the 6 figure annual family income in the course of their immigrant life in the USA.

But to think that it's just individual hard work and family saving that did the trick is to take credit for away from Korean-American communities.

Korean immigrants developed a financial support network that function like a bank in many ways. This was necessary because many banks in the USA would not take a chance on them when they needed to purchase their own buildings and equipment. Even if their English were flawless and they were able to prepare applications, they would most likely have been turned down. In most cases, they did not have enough equity in their house, if any, and their business ventures were too risky by any business loan standards in the USA. The fact that many succeeded does not minimize the risk factor when they were starting out. As Korean immigrants faced certain rejection for bank loans, they organized and formed financial associations.

The most wide-spread and effective financial association in the Korean-American community in the USA was the Lump-Sum System (called "Gae" in Korean). The "membership" in the system was determined by how much you could give per month. If you could give a $1,000 per month than you would join a $1,000-a-month Lump-Sum System. If you could give $500 per month, then you would join the $5000-a-month Lump-Sum System.

This is basically how it worked. If you joined a $1,000 per month Lump-Sum System made up of 20 members, every member would pay $1,000 per month. So, every month, $20,000 in cash were collected. The members decided who would collect the lump sum every month. So, in the period of 20 months, every person would collect $20,000 in lump sum.

The idea was that in order to buy a shop or a house, you need a lump sum deposit. Some people could not wait 20 months – how long it would take to save that on your own – for the deposit because the store that you wanted was going on sale in 3 months. You needed that lump sum then. Getting that store would guarantee increase of profit by 3 fold. Thus, you have an incentive to join this and get the $20,000 to put a down payment for that store in time. Paying a $1,000 per month after acquiring that store building would be easy because your profit would have increased by 3 times. In the long run, there is a profit.

If for some reason you became the 20th person to collect, which means that you could have saved on your own, it still will benefit you in the long run. This is the case because you have to remember that 20 members of the Lump-Sum System become bonded as colleagues. This functions as a business support group. If there were some emergencies, your Lump-Sum System group members are the best possibilities to seek help from.

Furthermore, the Lump-Sum System does not necessarily end with the first cycle. In more cases than not, they continue into second, third, fourth cycles, and even more. So, within 80 months (4 cycles), you are able to put a down-payment on a store, a down payment on a house, and then have two cycles left over for other things, such as buying a second or third store. Many Koreans branch out into owning 2-4 stores in a 20 year period after immigrating to the USA.

For many Korean-Americans, without the Lump-Sum System, they would not have been able to attain their $300,000 per year profit status in 20 years after immigrating to the USA with relatively nothing. The Korean community was able to organize effectively for communal and self-survival. Thus, Korean-Americans' ability to achieve their financial status stands as an immigration success story in the USA.

Of course, not all Koreans achieved 6 figure status in 20 years, but it would be safe to say that the majority of Korean-Americans would be seen as success stories by American economic standards. In fact, the first generation of Korean immigrants were so successful that many of their Harvard-educated children do not even come close to making the money that their parents have made with their broken English. Not a few holders of Ivy League MBA's have turned their backs on Wall Street to go work for their parents' "companies."

Indeed, the story of Korean-American parents working 13 hours per day for 6 days per week is common knowledge among Korean-Americans. Ivy League Koreans, now numbering in the thousands (as registered students), all have the commonality of the shared experience in knowing many Korean parents who fit the "type." Many can claim their own parents or grandparents as such a "type."

The reality of the economic struggles of Korean-American parents is embedded in the Korean-American collective memory. Hopefully, there will be more and more recounting and recording of this collective memory and experience.

Social Struggles of the Parents

Korean-American Experience in the United States

Economic struggles are not the only struggles that Korean immigrant parents faced after arriving in the USA. First generation Korean immigrants encountered many social problems. This is not surprising given the fact that most Korean immigrants had an idealized perception of America that did not jive with the reality of being immigrants in the USA. There are several reasons for the idealized picture of the American society.

First of all, most Koreans in the 70s and 80s perceived Americans as liberators and accorded America tremendous amount of respect. The reason for this is historical. After being occupied by Japan from 1910 to 1945, Koreans were liberated when the Americans dropped atomic bombs in Hiroshima and Nagasaki. If it were not for the VJ Day, Koreans would have continued in object colonialism. There were many horrible things that happened during the Japanese Occupation. For instance, Japanese colonizers forbade the Korean language and required Japanizing Koreans' names. Many from the generation of the Japanese Occupation cannot read or write Korean very well, while they are fluent in Japanese. Many had to learn Korean after the liberation.

For South Koreans, they experienced freedom again by American help during the Korean War. South Korea was almost completely taken over by the communist

North Korea, when General Douglas MacArthur successfully waged a military campaign. After the end of the Korean War, American soldiers came to be stationed in South Korea and there was active economic and political aid from the American government. Almost all the Koreans appreciated American presence and help after the Korean War.

The fact that American Christians sent missionaries to build schools, universities, and hospitals further created a positive impression for America in the popular psyche. Many American missionaries actually came in person and stayed their whole life in Korea, working with local Korean churches and pastors. This convinced the general Korean populace that Americans personally cared about Korea and Koreans. Why else would these white Americans come as missionaries with money support from churches in the USA, leaving behind a comfortable home in the USA for a war-devastated land of Korea?

The positive perception of Americans came to be deeply ingrained in the thinking and experience of the Korean people. It was not uncommon to go to the most rural village and find the villagers describing America in positive and glowing terms in the 60s, 70s, and 80s. Of course, there were other factors that helped the positive perception of America.

Another reason why Koreans generally have an idealized picture of America is due to the fact that America is economically advanced. American products entered the Korean market relatively quickly as the post-war Korean populace embraced America. American products were held up as the best and most desirable. Stories of American companies and technological achievement obtained mythic status as adults told the stories to children. Children in turn traded stories with each other like baseball cards. The American economic success was held up to be the standard to which everything was to be measured. American economic success became the goal for every Korean company and aspiring Korean youths.

Of course, the fact that Koreans viewed America in positive terms generally certainly paved the way to adoring American economic successes. This modern acceptance and respect stand in contrast to the first reception that the Americans received from the Koreans in the late 1800s. Koreans, including intellectuals, resisted American contact. In fact, Koreans killed the first missionaries and fired upon the first American ship. Thus, it would be most accurate to say that several factors worked together in symbiotic relationship to produce eventual idealization of America.

The third reason that helped positive perception of America was the fact that many Koreans went to America to study. Particularly, Christian organizations aggressively funded scholarships for Koreans to study in the USA. Many Christian churches and seminaries provided scholarships for Koreans to receive seminary training in the USA. The most noteworthy were the Baptists, although other Christian denominations were also very aggressive in funding Korean Christians to study in the USA. When the first waves of graduates of Koreans from American universities and seminaries returned to Korea, they quickly took leadership positions in Korean government, education, society, and churches. Most of these Korean leaders were aggressively pro-American.

Although most Christian organizations providing scholarships did not have an active interest in producing pro-American sentiment, the result of their scholarships had a long-lasting effect in Korea in the direction of favoring America. It can even be argued that the money was not the most important factor for a push toward pro-Americanism. American missionaries who worked in South Korea and passed on the scholarships on behalf of Baptist (or other) churches in America acted as genuine friends.

American friendship was clear in the holistic approach to evangelism and missions in South Korea. Christian organizations providing scholarships also provided moral support. The Korean recipient of a scholarship knew that there were people rooting for them and praying for them. They were sent letters by supporting churches in America. Some Korean students were even invited into the homes of American church members who supported them financially. The personal touch to the funding support that Koreans received endeared the American people to them.

But perhaps the most significant reason why Koreans came to idealize America can be found in the fourth reason. Koreans came to idealize America as Christianity grew in number and influence in the Korean society. Christianity grew in Korea like wildfire with the result that eventually Korea came to have the world's biggest Presbyterian church (almost 100,000 members) and the world's biggest charismatic church (almost 1,000,000 members).

The American Baptist stamp can be clearly seen in all Korean Christian denominations, and almost every Korean Christian pastor speaks of American Christianity in glowing terms. Korean churches sought to model their Christian piety and worship along American evangelical Christian lines, regardless of the denomination.

The fact that American Baptists, particularly from the southern states, poured generous money in educating Koreans certainly was a catalyst. Even today, Dallas Theological Seminary is held up as the model for Christian seminary training that combines theological learning with Christian piety. Many of the Christian living standards taught in Dallas Theological Seminary became the standard in almost all Korean Christian denominations. Rev. Billy Graham became the single most respected living clergy in Korea.

Koreans studying in America were genuinely impressed by the aggressive evangelistic zeal of American Baptists. The evangelistic model of the Baptists were standardized and internalized in Korean Christian churches with the success rate akin to the American Baptist movement in driving up the membership numbers. Fire-and-Brimstone preaching became very popular. Moody Bible Institute type focus on Christian education was held up as the operative model for educating the laity.

In Korean culture drinking is perceived as the way to cement social relations, but the drinking emphasis has also been identified as a primary cause for many social problems. Thus, the teetotaler American Baptist culture and its accompanying radical holiness movement came to be respected and identified as the way to move the Korean society forward and upwards. The

Korean-American Experience in the United States

Puritan self-control of American Baptists shocked many Koreans and won them over.

In fact, every Korean church has testimonies of how an American Baptist type pietism saved marriages, families, and individuals. Since many Koreans found contentment and happiness through American Baptist type of pietistic philosophy, it was natural to hold America as the spiritual role model and leader. As Koreans came to respect American evangelical Christians, they came to hold up America as a Christian country worthy of respect that Jesus and his apostles received. Since many Koreans came to value their Christian identity as the most important, their Christian commitment cemented loyalty toward America and idealization of America. America was the Christian Promised Land.

As America took on an epic picture as the model Christian nation in the mentality of devoted Korean Christians, many of whom came to be very influential in Korean society in all areas, America benefited from the domino effect of positive perceptions. America could not do any wrong. Even the most anti-Christians were influenced by aggressive pro-American agenda of Christian leaders in Korean society. More importantly, Korean Christians, concentrated in the lowest and poorest classes in the Korean society, provided a popular mandate of pro-American support.

In other words, pro-American agenda of Korean Christians in elite positions was backed up by popular support of working classes who converted to Christianity and testified how Christianity (American Baptist type of piety) saved their families from the negative forces of alcohol consumption and gambling. Like the American Baptists of the time, Korean Christians aggressively preach against alcohol consumption of any kind and gambling in any forms. This is the case with Korean churches in the Korean Diaspora. For instance, the prohibition on alcohol consumption is clearly in effect in Cambridge Open Church, the Korean Christian congregation meeting in Holy Trinity Church, Cambridge.

It is a truism to say that many Koreans came to view America as the Holy Land and the Land of the Promise. America is perceived to be the closest thing to heaven on earth. Thus, most Koreans went to the USA, thinking that it was a good place, a decent place, where children can be raised to be good and honorable. America was seen as a place where honest hard work will result in reaping positive benefits and wealth by legitimate means. The American Dream mixed with ideals of Christianity came to have a magical power over the perceptions of Koreans immigrating to the USA.

Korean-American Experience in the United States

Of course, when Korean immigrants arrived in the USA, they did not find heaven on earth. There were many difficult experiences and disappointments. But fundamentally, Korean immigrants were not able to get rid of their ideal perception of America. Koreans in the USA fundamentally believed in the American Dream even as they experienced difficulties. It was a faith which was not tangible, and to a certain extent it was illogical. But this faith in America as the Promised Land gave Koreans hope that most likely gave them strength in times of the greatest difficulties. And difficulties that Korean immigrant parents faced were numerous and often intense.

There are many social difficulties that Korean-American parents faced after arriving in America. Some of the difficulties that Korean-Americans experienced share much in common with the experiences of other immigrants in America. There is a certain amount of social resistance on the part of proceeding immigrant communities to accept the newer immigrant community.

For instance, when the Italians came over in droves after the Irish immigration, there was wide-spread conflict between Italian and Irish communities. Some members of the Irish community derided newer Italian immigrants with derogatory titles and gave them a hard time. Some Irish immigrants actively and explicitly discouraged their daughters from marrying Italians. And there were other types of violent exclusions.

To be fair, however, it is important to mention that there were some in the Irish community who embraced newer immigrants with open arms. But the general trend, whether it is with the Irish, Italians, or another immigration community, was to experience difficulties in social realms at the hand of preceding immigrants whose community has become more established – certainly more than the newer immigrant community. The case was no different with the Korean immigration community. Many Korean immigrants suffered at the hand of preceding, more established immigrant communities.

Besides experiencing unpleasantness by the preceding immigrant communities, Korean immigrants suffered on a general social level as well. There are two main reasons for this. First of all, because of the Vietnam War, there was general dislike of Vietnamese people. Not every Vietnam vet is anti-Vietnamese, but there is enough dislike of Vietnamese people in America that those who may look Vietnamese can suffer social discrimination.

Certainly, there are clear visible differences between Koreans and the Vietnamese people as there are clear differences between Spanish people and

Germans. But those in the larger society who have prejudices against the Vietnamese people generally do not take the time to study the differences. This social reality is quite clear in Koreans receiving the pejorative title "gook" that is meant for the Vietnamese people.

Secondly, Koreans have suffered at a general American social level because Koreans are mistakenly taken as Chinese. This is evident in the application of the pejorative term for the Chinese people – "chink" – for Koreans. Understanding from historical pers-pectives, it is possible to see what points resulted in anti-Chinese sentiment in America. While the Cold War was directed primarily at Russia, the fact that China was communist caused a type of hate-by-association. The term "red commies" or "red Chinese" was applied liberally in popular settings as well as in more polite society. Because some in the general American society perceived Korean immigrants as Chinese, Koreans suffered attacks meant for the Chinese in the midst of anti-Communist discourse.

Discrimination was not the only way Korean immigrants suffered socially. A primary factor in terms of social suffering was in the form of social exclusion. It is not uncommon to see recent Korean immigrants invited to functions held on a more general social level, like neighbourhood parties. A part of the reason for social exclusion is the problem of language communication. It is true that many Korean immigrants were not very good in English when they first arrived in the USA. But there are Korean immigrants who are relatively fluent or proficient in English. The fact of their exclusion may be identified in other factors.

First, Korean food uses exotic Asian spices. Many in the general American society do not like exotic Asian spices. There have been complaints of Asians smelling bad. The "bad smell," in fact, is associated with unfamiliarity with Asian spices. Since cooking with Asian spices generally imprints Asian spice smell on clothes, some Asians are accused of "smelling bad" (or smelling like Asian spices). Some in the general society find this unpleasant enough so they exclude, Asians, including Koreans, from social functions.

Secondly, some have difficulty with cultural differences. The Korean culture is quite different from the European-based culture. Korean culture, like Chinese culture, is Confucian with a cultural history expanding thousands of years. Because the Confucian culture is so different from the European-based culture, some in American culture want to ignore the whole cultural minefield by not inviting Asians to social functions.

Some figure that chances that things can go horribly wrong is far greater than the possibility for the success of a social function even with the most cautious attention to the social permutation. Trying to avoid a possible social disaster should not be confused with attitudes of intolerance, of course. But the end result is social exclusion. And sometimes, the lack of cultural knowledge and resulting exclusion socially have negative effects on the immigrant community. If, in fact, we hold up social participation as a value in and of itself, the fact of social exclusion can be seen innately to be negative – as a social suffering.

There are other ways Korean-American parents suffer socially. But perhaps the greatest social suffering in the new land is not inflicted by non-Koreans, but by Koreans. More specifically, Korean-American parents suffer socially as a result of what their children do or not do.

In order to understand Korean-American parents' suffering as the result of their children, it is important to examine the Korean-American youth experience on its own terms. In this spirit, I will devote the next section to explaining the experiences of Korean-American youths in America, including the difficulties they themselves face.

Korean Youth in America

The difficulty facing the Korean immigrant community extends to the children as well. But ironically, the biggest complaint among Koreans growing up in immigrant families is directed often at their parents. The complaint takes many forms but is essentially the same in nature. They are best expressed in sayings, such as "My parents don't love me" or "All they care about is their business." Essentially, many Korean youths complain about the lack of time that their parents spend with them. They often interpret this as lack of love.

This complaint highlights the cultural divide that marks the first generation of immigrants and the following generation. The first generation of immigrants never consider the possibility of being accused of not loving their kids. In fact, they had moved halfway across the world for the benefit of their kids and their future. All they were doing in the USA was for the benefit of the kids. They were willing to endure cultural shock, societal discomfort and even harassment, in order to ensure a bright future for their kids. Knowing that they were opening up possibilities for their kids often gave them hope in the midst of despair and many hours of work.

Thus, it is not surprising to find many Korean parents utterly shocked when they find out that their kids believe that their parents don't love them. For many of them, that was the last thing that they expected to hear. Obviously, there was a breakdown of communication. Somehow, the knowledge of the fact that their parents love them has not been transferred to the children.

There are several reasons for this problem. The greatest reason, perhaps, is the cultural gap. Social values of what constitutes love are different in Korea and in the USA. In Korea, love is expressed through actions, rather than verbally enumerated. Thus, in Korea parents working long hours are assumed to be the evidence of love for their kids. Why else would parents toil many laborious hours if it were not for the kids? On the other hand, American social values emphasize spending time with the kids as the evidence of showing love. If parents loved their kids, they would spend time with them and make time for them in the midst of a busy schedule. Clearly, working hard does not indicate love in and of itself.

Korean parents who immigrate to the USA operate from the Korean model. That is the model by which they were raised by their parents. And this is the worldview they grew with. By their worldview firmly entrenched in their adult psyche, they operate vis-à-vis their children. This is how they define parental love. For Korean immigrant parents, working hard in and of itself constitutes clear show of love, and they expect their children to understand it. To a certain extent, they are assuming that their children operate from the same cultural matrix.

However, many Korean children's worldviews are significantly altered as they enter American society and are educated by American institutions. Korean youths learn that love means spending time together. This American idea of parental love is advanced in television, particularly in episodes that deal with the topic. Often, coming to America at an early age, Korean immigrant children are readily acculturated into this framework of thinking. It is not an active process of cultural adoption. Rather, without noticing, Korean immigrant children hold their parents up by the standards set in television programs.

It is not just popular media in the USA that emphasizes the idea of parents spending time together as a chief evidence of love. Even in formal education in schools, this idea is implicitly upheld and even actively taught. When parents do not show up to parents' meetings or when children say that they do not spend much time with their parents, teachers assume that there is a problem at home. More often than not, teachers will assume that the parents are not being good parents and give enough love for their kids. Some teachers might even express this verbally.

Growing up in the American cultural matrix, Korean immigrant children come to build up resentment against their parents, more often than not. By the cultural standards of America, Korean immigrants are found guilty. On one level, you cannot blame the Korean children from developing this value system. They are immersed into the American cultural system and engage it actively as children and youth by many media available to them.

And more often than not, they have no other information to offset it. In other words, many Korean youths do not have alternate sources of information that challenges the standards of judgement set by the American society. In this regard, parents might have to take some blame. Perhaps, they need to find channels to share their cultural values.

Another factor that may require greater attention is "neglect." Many Korean parents do not explain that they are working hard for their children's benefit. Not only do they assume that their children know, they are embarrassed to communicate this to them. Korean culture is not a verbally expressive culture when it comes to matters such as this. Many children become healthy adults without even hearing that their parents love them. Sentiments of love are often not expressly communicated in Korean culture on a general level, and this is no different in parent-children relationship.

Besides the cultural barriers from being communicative and expressive about their love for their kids, many Korean immigrants work many hours to stay afloat. Often, Korean parents leave home early to work and return home late from work. Practically, this does not leave much time for sitting down for a chat. Depending on the age of the Korean youths, the little time that Korean-American parents can find to chat is their bed time, homework time, or time to chat on the phone with friends.

But time is not the only problem. Many Korean-American immigrant parents work in physically demanding, labor intensive work for many hours. By the time they reach home, they are physically and mentally exhausted. Even if they have the mind to talk to their kids about how much they love them, they will find the task too emotionally challenging in the state that they are in. But more often than not, Korean-American parents assume that the children see them coming back late from work as self-revelatory of their love, so they do not bother to talk about the issue. For the children, the very fact that their parents do not seem to bother talking to them or spend time with them proves that their parents do not love them. There is certainly serious miscommunication here.

What often exasperates the miscommunication further is the kind of communication that transpires at the meeting points between the parents and the children. Whenever parents and children talk, it is invariably about school and studies. Parents ask if the children are doing well. They are visibly upset if their children bring home a bad grade. Parents are often pushing their children to go to an Ivy League university. From the parents' perspective, all this is showing parental concern. It was after all Korean-American parents' desire to see their children succeed that compelled them to come to the USA, so they want to see their children advance. Korean-American parents generally assume that good grades and good university are the secrets to success in the USA, so they push their children. They believe that they are doing this for their children's sake and because they love them.

American-educated Korean-American immigrant children see this as nagging, like their other American peers would. Having been brought up in the American society that sees the relationship between parents and children in different terms, Korean-American immigrant children often perceive typical Korean-American parents' questions about school as somehow infringing on their person and space. What often aggravates the conflict is that Korean-American parents often take an aggressive tone, typical of Korean parents vis-à-vis their children, which Korean immigrant children see as "wrong" – in light of what is portrayed in American media and in American social settings. Often, many Korean youths see themselves as emotionally scarred from these episodes. And Korean-American parents feel that they have been mistreated by their kids, who often end up being quite aggressive themselves, some even saying that their parents do not love them in very insulting manner.

Although cultural factors impede effective communication, perhaps the greatest obstacle for communication relates to language. Korean parents speak almost exclusively in Korean. What little English they pick up is what is associated with business and every day survival. Most Korean immigrants do not have a chance to practice English as their friends are normally Korean immigrants. In contrast, their children learn English very quickly as they attend school daily. Also, TV and movies encourage them to replace Korean with English as the primary language of reference and communication. Most Korean children learn English quickly and forget Korean.

As the language gap grows, it becomes harder and harder for Korean parents and their children to hold a meaningful conversation. The general pattern for parents and children communicating is children speaking increasingly broken Korean to parents who talk in Korean. Soon, children respond almost exclusively in English to their Korean parents who speak primarily Korean with them.

It is understandable why Korean language schools have proliferated in America. Korean parents desire better communication with their children, so they generously support Korean schools that instruct in Korean language, history, and culture training. Often, the practical necessity of daily work of many hours prohibits Korean parents from acquiring English language training on formal levels.

It is the practicalities of immigrant life that adds to the problem between Korean-American parents and their children. This problem of communication is quite wide-spread and can even be seen as a collective experience of the Korean-American community to a certain extent. However, miscommunication with their parents is only a part of the problem that Korean immigrant children face. Although Korean immigrant children may blame their parents primarily, their problems as children of immigration are much more complex. Many Korean children face great hurdles in American society that often leave them with emotional scars.

Perhaps, the greatest damage is done in schools. Many Korean immigrant children experience cultural and social hardship in American schools, and more than a few of them are left with lasting emotional scars. Besides damages from cultural shocks, Korean immigrant children suffer from the general American capitalist standards of what is cool and what is not. To be in the accepted group, often minimal clothing style standards are required. Clothes and shoes that would be socially respected in the peer group is often expensive. This is not surprising since commercialism and capitalism often play an important role in defining the cool factor.

Many new Koran immigrants cannot afford designer clothes and designer shoes, so from the beginning, Korean immigrant children are placed in the uncool category. Often, Korean immigrant children take time to adapt to their surrounding and understand what helps for social acceptance. Even when Korean immigrants figure this out, neither they nor their parents can afford the items that they need. So, understanding does not necessarily mean acceptance.

Like other children being placed in the uncool category on account of need, Korean immigrant children often develop resentment and low self-esteem. And in the society that is very American, their uncool status opens them up to social criticism and peer harassment. Just like in the movies where "cool" kids put "uncool" kids in lockers or hang them up in bathrooms, not a few Korean immigrant kids have experienced physical harassment. The only factor that saves some Korean kids is the fact that they learned Taekwondo. Having watched many martial arts T.V. shows and movies, many American kids develop a fear for someone who knows martial arts. Many Korean immigrant kids are able to use this to their advantage to survive attacks reserved for "uncool" kids.

But the general standards for all adolescents are not the only obstacles Korean immigrant kids face. As immigrants, Korean-Americans face further social stigmatization. Often, Koran immigrant kids are ridiculed for not being able to speak English well and for speaking English with a Korean accent. Although some Korean immigrant kids escape the most cruel settings, more often than not, Korean immigrant kids face social ostracization for being Korean immigrants.

The reaction to this type of ostracization is one of two kinds, generally. Some Korean immigrants withdraw into themselves. Korean kids spend time studying or pouring themselves into practicing a musical instrument. This effort away from socializing with American students is helped, perhaps inadvertently, by Korean parents, who often encourage their children to study or excel at an instrument. Many Korean kids, therefore, become excellent students and performers of musical instruments. This reality is so widespread that one of the stereotypes for Korean kids is that they receive good grades and play an instrument. According to kids' lingo, a typical Korean-American would be a "geek." This label further stigmatizes Korean immigrant kids in the American setting.

The other common reaction to general social ostracization that Korean immigrant kids experience is to develop friendship mostly with Koreans. As Korean immigrants befriend only Korean immigrants, this often slows down their ability to acculturate into the American society and culture. In the short run and in the long run, this social development among Korean immigrant kids becomes problematic in their progress in the American society. Since Korean immigrant kids have permanently moved to the USA, their lack of non-Korean American friends can be a serious problem for them in the long-run. But their befriending only Korean immigrant kids can be understood on psychological grounds. It is a defense mechanism in the midst of larger American society ostracization of immigrants.

Often, the problem is not confined to peer ostracization. Many Korean immigrant kids experience a type of discrimination by their teachers. Perhaps, the teachers of the Korean immigrant kids do not purposely discriminate against Korean kids. Some of it might be ingrained in the culture that gives immigrants a hard time. Or unknowingly, they have become a part of institutional racism. This is what some have come to call "internalized discrimination." These teachers are a part of the larger society and its prejudices against people who are different.

Unless they actively work against it, it would not be difficult for teachers to fall victim to negative societal trends. Realistically, it is difficult to require every teacher to be consciously on-guard against internalized stereotypes and discrimination. Although it is impossible for humans to be superhuman in this regard, it does not deny the fact that Korean immigrant kids are affected by it.

And certainly it is not altogether impossible to rule out a malicious discrimination of Korean immigrants by some American teachers on purpose. Evil exists in the world and some manifestations of evil is expected in humanity. And such practices of exclusion have characterized the human race for centuries, regardless of culture and nationality. Korean immigrant kids who experience this type of malicious treatment by American teachers often develop emotional scars that last a life time.

Korean-American Experience in the United States

The Korean-American community has yet to address this problem that exists in the community. Often, the fact that Korean-American parents do not experience this particular form of mistreatment does not help their children who suffer. The fact that many Korean parents emphasize respecting of teachers in the Korean fashion sometimes aggravates their children who may suffer. Sometimes, therefore, a type of aggressive reaction to their non-Korean teachers might become redirected at their parents. This sometimes adds to the friction already existent between Korean immigrant parents and their children.

Korean children in America often experience further suffering as immigrants. Often, this takes the form of discrimination based on color. As Koreans are visibly different from the American white majority, this causes them to be easy targets for discrimination. Whereas Irish and Polish immigrants can soon find acceptance by general white majority as they are socialized into American society and educated in the USA, Korean immigrants are visibly different and this does not allow for full integration.

Even in cases where Koreans experience complete cultural adaptation and attain highest education in the USA, the fact that Korean immigrants look visibly different is a stumbling block to full acceptance.

This problem based on color is quite pronounced in the USA, particularly in non-Christian settings. And this problem persists throughout generations. Thus, a Korean who belongs to the fourth or fifth generation will experience this type of unacceptance in the USA even if she speaks in perfect English and cannot speak Korean or have even been to Korea. Many Koreans have been asked questions, such as, "No, no, where are you really, originally from?"

Perhaps, this problem associated with color or visible difference from the white majority will never go away. Certainly for now, it does play a major role in Korean immigrant experience and self-awareness. Problems associated with color often contribute to negative memory, both on an individual and collective levels.

For Korean children of immigration, the experience of discrimination based on color is more pronounced because of their active engagement with the larger culture in academic settings. As many Korean-American youths eventually end up working in job settings where they comprise the very few people of color, they will most likely continue to experience this type of discrimination.

Thus, Korean-American youths of immigration experience problems of their own that they feel keenly, and these problems become an integral part of their person. They are often made aware of the problems through personal reflection, experience, and reading relevant materials, such as produced by the civil rights movement. In their personal journey for awareness, these children of immigration often leave their parents behind. Parents of immigration do experience discrimination, but often they miss the subtleties inherent in the American culture and in the discourse. Therefore, they are not as affected by them in such a deep way. Korean-American children, in contrast, have become better sensitized to the American cultural subtext which allows them to experience discrimination at a heightened level of awareness.

Not being able to communicate on the same wavelength with their parents about their experiences and pains leave many Korean immigrant children with a sense of isolation and loneliness. Some Korean immigrant children have been reluctant to discuss these topics with other Korean-American immigrants for fear that their experience might be isolated. They may be afraid of what their Korean friends might think of them. It is only very recently that Korean-American children of immigration have begun to explore their feelings and experiences. Being in the beginning stages of expression, one would be hard-pressed to find much literature on this issue.

Unfortunately, the Korean community in the USA has not been particularly supportive of exploring these issues so far, although there is a glimmer of hope for change. The reason for the relative silence on the matter is that it is not a part of the Korean cultural experience to air grievances publically or devote research funds to exploring painful collective experiences. Most Koreans feel that it is better to bury the past and forget painful experiences. Being able to "move on" from painful experiences has made Koreans adept survivors in any setting and forward-looking in their enterprises. The problem is that history and collective experiences are not given the treatment that they deserve. In a way, the problem relates to the value of historical record and the preservation of human experiences.

Things are prone to change in this regard in the future as many children of immigration have fully reached their adult success stage and would be willing to fund research specifically in this regard. In other words, it is their own experiences that can motivate funding for research on this topic.

Another positive note in this regard is that American-born children of immigration are beginning to consciously develop self-awareness and are actively discussing these topics. And unlike their parents before them, the Korean-American children of immigration are more willing to encourage their children's interest in investigating sociological questions facing the Korean-American community and individuals. As Korean immigrant communities have attained greater financial security and social security, members of the Korean-American community are more willing to allow their children to "indulge" in the quest for identity and understanding.

Of course, next few decades will tell to what extent the Korean-American self-awareness has been raised. The publications in the following years will show the social consciousness in the Korean-American community in the USA.

The Great Korean Tragedy

Perhaps the single most traumatic experience in Korean history is the Japanese occupation of Korea (1910-1945). The Japanese regime had the blessing of European powers to colonize Koreans. To a certain extent, Koreans are not freed from guilt since they did not proactively prevent diplomatic efforts by Japan to win international support for its occupation program.

That is not to say that official Korean delegation was not sent. They were. But they were not effective in winning any diplomatic wars on behalf of Korea. By the time Japan treacherously occupied Korea, they had done so with the approval and cooperation of European national powers. And the years of occupation were horrible ones.

The harms of occupation is self-evident. A foreign power enslaving the local population for several decades can easily transform the character of a people. As the colonialist power, Japan occupied much territory and stole land and property from Koreans. Many Korean grandparents can give living testimonies as to how Japan tried to execute their occupation plans to maximize benefit for Japan and the Japanese people. Power was conscientiously and deliberately taken away from the Korean people. The efforts to self-determination were cruelly suppressed.

But besides typical enslavement tactics and human rights violations associated with colonialist occupation and managing occupied territories, Japan went beyond even what is typical for an occupying power. Japan forced Koreans to change their names. It was not a voluntary act of the Korean people. They did not choose to change their names in order to get ahead in their professions or to be better accepted in society. The change of name was forced upon the Korean people. It was clearly a tactic by the occupying Japanese people to break the Korean people and force them to submit to Japan.

Japan utilized other efforts to break the Korean spirit. Japan forced Koreans to speak only Japanese. Japanese was taught in Korea's schools, and the teaching of Korean was suppressed by the force of law with a visible display of occupational colonialist power. Many Koreans during this stage grew up not learning to read or write Korean as they were not taught in schools. Korean parents often broke the law by requiring their children to speak Korean at home. These popular efforts helped to maintain the Korean language as the vernacular of the Korean people. This was, however, a small victory as the colonialist program succeeded in replacing formal education in the occupied territories.

Although many Koreans protested Japanese occupation inwardly, many failed to protest visibly and audibly. Colonialist programs of Japan in the occupied Korea, in essence, did break the Korean spirit as seen in the fact that Koreans were not able to mount a protest or revolt of their own with any extensive level of success. Even the most effective protest, the March 1st Movement, proved to be quite ineffective in denting the Japanese colonialist program. The freedom of Korea was delivered to Korea by the United States, which had purchased their freedom by dropping two atomic bombs in Japan. The fact that the Korean people did not win their freedom on their own will undoubtedly have long-lasting repercussions in Korean history.

The Japanese Occupation was a horrible event in history and it effectively destroyed the fighting spirit of the Korean people and sanitized them as a model colonized people. When one examines the kind of ruthless tactics that Japan used, it might not be difficult to understand the psychological damage done to Korea and Koreans that effectively paralyzed the Korean people.

One of the ruthless tactics that Japan used can be seen in the "Comfort Women." The Japanese government took the most beautiful women from Korean families and shipped them off to be prostitutes for the

Japanese soldiers. It is not difficult to imagine the anger and pain that this produced in the Korean women who were shipped off to Japanese soldiers like merchandise. The sense of empathy and loss the families felt must have been great.

    The tragedy accentuated by the reality of the Comfort Women was that neither the women nor their families could do anything about it. Japan was the occupying power and they had proven ruthless. Japan showed that they did not respect the lives of Korean people and often killed Koreans at will. When their daughters were shipped off to be prostitutes for the Japanese army, their families could do nothing but watch. Any protest could have meant certain and painful death. Japan already had complete power over Korea when the Comfort Women were shipped off.

    One can almost begin to imagine the sense of helplessness that these Koreans felt. There were thousands of Comfort Women from all over Korea. There was, therefore, a feeling of helplessness that pervaded the Korean communities, which were unable to help the women or their families. The sense of guilt and helplessness further immobilized the Korean society and the Korean people from asserting their freedom and will. Koreans were not only militarily occupied, they were psychologically subdued and dehumanized.

Although the Comfort Women incident stands as a monument of colonialist oppression and abuse by Japan, it is certainly not the only one. Japan also carried out a programmic oppression of Korean Christians. Japan, being the most friendly of Asian countries towards western countries, understood the revolutionary power of Christianity. Japan understood that Christianity could be dangerous in installing a sense of self-respect and popular dignity. Japan understood the fierce wars fought and won by Christians in the west. Japan understood that if Korean Christians were unchecked, then they would become the undoing of the Japanese Occupation.

And Japan vigorously attacked Korean Christians and stepped up their persecution with every advancing year of occupation. Japan tried many intimidation tactics. Perhaps the most remembered collectively is the boarding of churches by Japanese soldiers while Korean Christians were worshipping inside. As Korean Christians sang hymns of praise to Christ, they were burned alive.

Not only did Japan persecute Korean Christians as a group, there were many targeted persecution of individual Korean Christians. Particularly, the Korean clergy was targeted because the rationale was that if they could get Korean ministers to renounce their Christian faith, then they could get his church members to renounce their Christian loyalty. Perhaps, the most famous of the Korean clergy who was publically persecuted the Japanese government was Rev. Ju, Ki-Chul. He refused to renounce his faith to Christ and was imprisioned and tortured. Most remembered is the Japanese government forcing Rev. Ju to walk on a bed of nails. As this was done publically, Rev. Ju's church members sang the hymn, "I Go Towards That Heavenly Place." Rev. Ju was ultimately martyred for his Christian faith.

There were many others, and some of them suffered in silence and died in loneliness without anyone to sing hymns to encourage them. Many of the Korean Christian martyrs during the Japanese Occupation were tortured before they were killed. As the Japanese government was interested in breaking the Christian spirit in Korea, they were more interested in getting the majority of Christians to renounce their Christian faith more than killing a few dedicated Christians.

Some of the ways in which Korean Christians were tortured include being hung upside down and having a soup made of spicy red hot chilly peppers poured down their nose. Some were forced to be submergeed in icy river or lake in winter time. There were many more cruel ways in which Korean Christians were tortured.

The Japanese government was often unsuccessful in causing their victims to renounce their Christian faith. Perhaps, their error from the logistic point of view is that they often targeted models of Christian faith who rose to the occasion and showed what Christian faith they were made of.

However, the Japanese government had one very important and far-reaching victory. Conversely, it was a blow to Koreans. The Japanese government threatened the General Assembly of the only Korean Presbyterian denomination at the time and procured their support.

Basically, the Korean Presbyterian Church was faced with the choice (presented by the Japanese government) of putting the Japanese Shinto shrines in their worship sanctuaries and being left alone or rejecting the Japanese Shinto shrines and facing military persecution.

From the Japanese side, it is understandable why Japan was willing to leave Korean churches alone if they placed Japanese Shinto shrine in their worship sanctuary. Japan knew enough about Christianity that they understood that allowing Japanese Shinto Shrines into the Christian worship room was tantamount to corrupting Christianity. They understood that it was compromising the historic Christian faith that emphasizes that the Triune God of the Bible is the only one true God. "Thou shall have no other gods before me" stands as a key command from the Ten Commandments. Japan understood from the history of Christianity and from Christian texts that Christianity in Korea would be compromised and their spirit effectively curtailed if Korean churches were willing to put Japanese Shinto shrines in their sanctuaries.

Furthermore, Japan understood that placing a Japanese Shinto shrine in the inner sanctuary of worship represented acknowledgement of the supremacy of Japan over Korea. In other words, it was a political symbol as well. Japan would have been content with this symbolic gesture. By putting Shinto shrines in the inner sanctum of Christian worship, Koreans were selling their souls to Japan.

It is undoubtable that many Korean Presbyterian clergy at the General Assembly understood the compromise they were making. But it is possible that some made the compromise with honest, good intentions (at least in their minds). One of the arguments was that it is better to save the lives of the church members so that they can continue to worship Jesus than reject the Japanese threat and put their lives in danger. A saying goes that the road to Hell is paved with good intentions. Certainly, in terms of compromising the Korean spirit from resisting Japanese colonialism, the Presbyterian clergy effectively helped the Japanese occupying power even if they did not "really" intend to do so.

The vote by the General Assembly was a major victory for the occupying Japanese forces because the decision came to be binding on all member churches.

Perhaps, it should be noted here that the General Assembly was held in North Korea (before Korea was divided into two). Many of the clergy voting to support the measure had churches in North Korea. Some have explained subsequent misfortune that fell on North Korea after the Independence Day as resulting from their actions during the Japanese Occupation.

After the Independence, there were Christian students who took it upon themselves to repent for the sins of the Christians who compromised Christ and the body of Christ (the Christian church). This student initiated prayer and repentance movement came to be called the Student For Christ (SFC) movement. The SFC movement is evidence that among the Korean populace there was the recognition of a wrong done in the decision of the General Synod that corrupted a part of Korean Christianity. It was a popular movement started by the masses. Almost 60 years later, over 20,000 students meet in a national SFC conference in Korea.

The Japanese Occupation was a horrible time in Korean history when a lot of compromise was committed. Not only did these church leaders compromise, many Korean society leaders compromised. The Japanese government compelled, coaxed, paid, and forced Korean society leaders to collaborate with the occupying Japanese power. For one reason or other, many Korean societal leaders compromised and became hired agents of the Japanese regime.

Logistically, it would have been impossible for the Japanese occupying forces to rule the Korean people if they did not have help from the Korean collaborators. There were millions of Koreans to several thousand Japanese troops. The fact that so many Korean societal leaders willingly helped the Japanese regime stands as a mystery and shame for the Korean people. What is more embarrassing is the fact that it was the educated, who should have been providing moral and logistic leadership for the Korean people, who sold out the Korean people. The spirit of the Korean people was effectively compromised during the Japanese Occupation. Colonialist imprint has, therefore, left a lasting mark on the Korean society and the Korean psyche.

What are some of the noticeable imprints of Japanese colonialism on the Korean society and the Korean psyche? Perhaps, least tangible but most noticeable is the reluctance to engage the political and social power structure. There seems to be a fundamental fear of authority structures that is internalized. Even when power structures allow oppression to happen or do not aid in the protection of Koreans, Koreans are resigned to such a situation. It never seems to cause Koreans to consider ways to force the power structure to work for them.

A good case in point is found in the aftermaths of LA Riots. Many Korean businesses were ruined. Many Koreans in the Los Angeles area did not work hard to organize in order to claim from the state and other power structures the help that they needed to rebuild. Many Koreans took the suffering lying down. Many Koreans accepted the current state of disadvantage as the way things are as if it was meant to be that way by some cosmic design.

If Korean-Americans organized with the particular aim of compelling local, state, and federal government and social agencies to lend help, they could have easily succeeded in obtaining the needed help. But they were not able to organize. Perhaps, the reason why they were unable to organize is due to the fact that they did not have a clear, articulated goal to organize the community around. Perhaps, they believed that nothing could be done even if they organized. This kind of thinking would not be uncommon in the colonized mindset.

Often, when Koreans are asked about the need for positive social change, their response is that it will take two to three generation to change things. Perhaps, they are right. Some changes will actually take two to three generations. But it is their attitude that is telling. From the beginning, Koreans take a pessimistic view. It is a type of defeatism that accepts losses before even entering a context. In other words, saying that it will take two or three generations to change things is a euphemism for saying that it cannot be done in the period of one's life, so he will not worry about it or about working to change things. It is a way of relinquishing responsibility.

Of course, a sense of helplessness is different from the inability to organize to make positive changes. But two are invariably linked.

In order to bring about political or social change, Koreans have to organize. Koreans' inability to identify the ultimate goal and rally Koreans to reach that goal show a type of a defeated colonized spirit. It is not surprising considering that Japan worked for decades to break the Korean spirit during the period of Japanese colonialism.

Japan did a good job of creating a sense of helplessness and inability to motivate change. During the Japanese occupation, control was absolute and everywhere. This allowed atrocities such as the Comfort Women and Christian martyrdom. The feeling of helplessness to affect change even in the most important issues for the sake of those whom they cared most about created a sense of hopelessness and helplessness that became internalized in the Korean psyche. Most individual Koreans came to share this sense of helplessness vis-à-vis the power structure.

Furthermore, it is important to recognize that Japan was effective in its colonialist program in Korea precisely because they were efficient in preventing Koreans from organizing and uniting to affect change. For Japan, its ability to separate Koreans and set Koreans against Koreans were crucial for maintaining the occupied territories. The lack of coherent Korean resistance against Japanese colonialism is evidence enough that Japan succeeded. Having being programmed for disunity under the Japanese regime, Koreans came to internalize the inability to unite effectively against power structures for collective Korean advancement or liberation.

The internalized feeling of helplessness and the inability to organize effectively against the existent power structure is costing many Korean communities. If Koreans fail to strip themselves of the internalized programming under the Japanese colonialism, Koreans will continue to suffer and be unable to reap the benefits of a united front.

Particularly, since democracy hinges on a group's ability to unite, Koreans are at a particular disadvantage when they find themselves in foreign lands where democratic process reigns. Modern democracies have been programmed along the lines of laissez-faire capitalism, where the fittest survive at the expense of the unfit. In the current situation, Koreans are proving to be unfit as a group capable of organizing and advancing its needs and collective benefit for the future. Thus, in the face of conflict, Koreans face extreme disadvantage. It is becoming more and more important that Koreans learn to be a fit group able to work together for the Korean common good. Koreans' ability to do what will prove to be their survival method in a foreign democracy where they are already at a disadvantage due to their minority and immigrant status.

The feeling of helplessness inculcated during the Japanese Occupation does not merely affect organizational dynamics among Koreans. Often, individual Koreans have been conditioned to feel a sense of helplessness as an individual before a dominant power. Among most Koreans, there is a pervasive acceptance of power as being correct. In other words, the political or social authority is assumed to be right without any critical questioning. In cases in which political and social power are good, this does not become problematic, but in cases where political or social power prove to be abusive and harmful, this uncritical acceptance of power can prove disastrous. Particularly in foreign settings, uncritical attitude toward political and social power of the land often casts Koreans out of due process and receiving of rights that innately and implicitly owed to them by right.

To a certain extent, Koreans need to remember that Western legal system and political process is ordered under the Hegelian model. To every thesis, an antithesis is expected. And as a result, a compromise or synthesis is reached. If Koreans are unable to produce the expected antithesis then all the Koreans will suffer. Often, thesis is more extreme then the position itself because of the expectant antithesis. By in large, Koreans have not been very effective in producing the needed antithesis. This is evident when we view political process and Korean students' efforts to get better treatment of Koreans in universities.

Individual Koreans have known to suffer unfairly and sometimes unnecessarily because individual Koreans, who are affected, have not adequately digested the idea of Hegelian dialectics inherent in many western institutions. On a more harmless level for instance, when a company offers a Korean individual a salary with a job offer, most Koreans accept the first quote. As a standard practice in a Hegelian system, the first offer is the lowest possible offer, and companies generally expect the individual to demand a higher pay (in other words, an antithesis). Whereas most Americans inherently understand the Hegelian dialectics in the hiring process, most Koreans do not. Thus, Koreans often suffer a financial loss in relative terms.

The above example is relatively harmless because hired Korean does not really "suffer" greatly as a result of a pay that could be a little bit higher. The loss does not bring pain in real or symbolic terms in most cases. But there are examples where Koreans will suffer real pain as the result of being unable to play along the Hegelian model. A major problem is that Korean individuals have been trained under the colonialist system that the power is absolute and unnegotiable. With a colonized mindset, most Korean individuals have difficulty reprogramming themselves to perceive power as not absolute and inherently negotiable. Certainly, a sense of helplessness vis-à-vis power works to damage Koreans in such cases.

Another way Japanese colonialism of Koreans have adversely affected Korea is in the uncritical trust of foreign influence. Before the Japanese colonialism, Korea was known as the Hermit Kingdom because of its isolationist policy. Korea mistrusted all foreigners. The Japanese Occupation swung the pendulum in the opposite extreme.

For Japan to be successful as the occupying power, it was crucial to develop a sense of acceptance of foreign culture and influence. Without systematically desensitizing Koreans to foreign influence, Japan could not carry out its colonialist aims. Japan effectively programmed Koreans to drop all sense of critical assessment in regards to foreign influence.

Modern Korea is most open and vulnerable to foreign influences out of the Asian countries. In fact, Korea aggressively imports foreign influences, whether they be in terms of merchandise or culture. In some cases this has helped Korea, particularly in the area of economics. But such a radical openness has had adverse effects. In some sense, the negatives outweigh the positives.

Importing of foreign influence and culture has made the Korean society very unstable. In other words, it is difficult to point to Korea and identify "Korean culture" because so much of modern Korea is not necessarily very distinctively Korean. Foreign terminology and outlook have become pervasive in society. Traditional Korean norms have been quickly and willingly thrown out. One noticeable factor in the last decade is that most Korean young do not own traditional Korean clothing. This stands in sharp contrast to Indian youths, both in India and in the USA, who own traditional clothing that they wear on special occasions.

Of course, clothing is only a small indicator. However, it is symptomatic of the general cultural reality. This is the case in Korea as well as in India. In cultural influences as well as other types of influences, all things foreign are aggressively welcome.

The problem, of course, is that being aggressively open and adopting foreign things often make Koreans forget that Korea is fundamentally different in its character and 5,000 years of history from the place from which they are importing. The adverse effect that could arise in having influences not function smoothly in the Korean setting is not surprising. This would be the case in cultural realities as well as economic issues.

One is bound to wonder if what the Koreans call "The IMF Incident" owes something to this phenomenon. In an effort to adopt all things foreign, Korean economy imputed many foreign elements without careful attention to internal development and distinctive needs in the Korean context. If Koreans spent more attention to internal developments rather than aggressively importing foreign ideas and products, the IMF Incident would have been more easily avoided or at least minimized.

The adverse effect of too quickly adopting things foreign would be the same on an individual level as well as societal levels. There will be a sense of imbalance and instability. If the individual or community is not careful, this can produce adverse affect that can damage in critical and permanent ways.

The Korean inability to be more critical of foreign influences stems from the colonialist program of Japan that desensitized Korea. Koreans along individual and corporate levels have been programmed to adopt foreign influences uncritically.

The colonizing power Japan clearly exhibits a contrasting reality. Japan is really slow to give up things that are distinctively Japanese. Furthermore, Japan exhibits great critical thinking in the way it processes foreign influences. This is because Japan and the Japanese people did not undergo decades of systematic social programming as Koreans did under Japanese colonialism. Korea was the colonized; Japan was the one colonizing.

In the American setting, Korean adaptation of foreign influence has had both positive and negative effects. Positively, Korean-Americans have been more adept at assimilation than many of their other Asian counterparts. Many Korean-Americans live individually and separately in a non-Korean context and neighborhoods with a few or no Koreans even in cities that have tens of thousands of Koreans. No concerted effort is utilized to create a Korea-town or Korean living center in most areas. Adopting foreign influences without much thinking has helped Koreans to assimilate to American culture more easily.

However, there is an adverse affect to the assimilationist model. Individual Korean-Americans might have been effective in adapting to the American setting, but this does not mean that Koreans are genuinely accepted by the larger setting. Often, Koreans experience types of social ostracization and varying degrees of social discrimination. As much as Koreans were able to assimilate within the larger American setting, they were often not able to do it completely because of their background and history and color.

Even in cases where it is perhaps possible for total assimilation, the fact that Koreans look visibly different often attract discrimination. As people are most affected by the visual, the fact that Koreans are a people of color play a role in the discrimination Koreans experience.

And more than a few Korean-Americans experience discrimination. In this regard, the fact that Koreans did not form distinctive Korean towns or neighbourhoods could have worked to their disadvantage. There is safety in numbers, and there is power in concentrated Korean organizations.

The fact that Korean-Americans are spread out all over the city and that there are often only one or two Korean families in a given neighborhood makes Koreans vulnerable. In communities where discrimination is not openly practiced, this would not matter, but when a community is hostile, sparse population of Koreans makes Koreans particularly vulnerable and easy targets.

In the American setting, therefore, a type of acceptance of non-Korean influence (a kind of assimiliation model) makes individual Koreans more vulnerable. In turn, this makes Korean-American communities more vulnerable.

Thus, in light of the problem facing the people of color in the USA, it might be argued that the assimilationist model for Koreans has been more negative than positive. The aggressive assimilationist model can be traced, at least in significant part, to the radical openness to foreign influence inculcated by the colonizing Japanese power.

Another adverse effect of Japanese Occupation on Koreans can be found in what is akin to the Stockholm syndrome. The fact that Japanese culture and all things Japanese are very popular in Korea is indicative of this reality. Within a generation of the end of the Japanese colonialism, Korean populace embraced Japanese cultureal and social influences through commercial channels. Korean tourists poured their hard earned money into Japanese industry.

It can be said that Koreans are a very forgiving people or that they have a short-term memory. However, it is recognizable that a factor not dissimilar to the Stockholm syndrome played a role in Koreans embracing their former tormentors. Certainly, the fact that the Japanese government had a systematic program of forcing Koreans to adopt Japanese ways with their colonialist power played a role in breaking down Korean defenses. Also, as the one in power, Japan integrated some of their Japanese ways into Korean culture, almost internalizing Japanese values into Korean mores.

The proof is in the reality. Many of the current Korean food are Japanese. There was introduction and imposition of Japanese food into Korean cuisine during the occupation period. It can be seen as a part of the program to subjugate or even destroy Korean culture. Food is a very important part of any culture.

The systematic program of intimidation, belittlement, and cunning play to deprive Koreans of their cultural identity by imputing Japanese elements was somewhat effective. The aftermath of Japanese colonialism can be seen as one in which Koreans lost the defensive pride in the Korean culture and norms. The colonialist program to force Koreans to adopt and like Japanese culture left a residue. Thus, soon after the end of Japanese colonialism, Koreans embraced Japanese ways. For most Koreans, sushi and Japanese noodles are among the most popular today.

This type of Stockholm syndrome has become applicable in today's context. For instance, if a Korean is harmed or adversely affected by non-Koreans, in many cases, Korean victims will start making excuses for the aggressor. The Korean victim often takes responsibility for the aggression unjustly inflicted.

This happens on a collective level. When a Korean is victimized by a non-Korean, often Koreans around the Korean victim will start justifying the aggressor and finding reasons to excuse the aggressor. Koreans often let the non-Korean aggressor down easy.

Such exercise from liability is not applied to the Korean victim. Other Koreans blame the Korean victim in some cases. Koreans often assume the fault must lie with the Korean victim and not the non-Korean aggressor. Surely, this point of view reflects a low self-esteem on a Korean communal level. A Korean cannot do right while a non-Korean is always right. One can see how the colonialist program of blaming Koreans for the Japanese colonialist fault would avoid wide-spread revolt against

Japanese occupation. In other words, programming Koreans to blame themselves or a member of their community would be self-destructive for Koreans but would provide longevity to those colonizing Koreans.

The kind of mentality currently extant in the Korean community is akin to the mindset of certain communities to blame the raped girl rather than the rapist. Some in the community might say that the girl must have done something wrong to be raped. Such statements incriminate the victim and exonerate the criminal.

In such communities, even the raped girl might be brainwashed into thinking that she did something wrong rather than gaining the mental power to blame the perpetrator. One can see how destructive this kind of mentality is for the victim and for the community in which the victim might be found. It would be hard to check the process of victimization against such a self-defeating community.

To a certain extent, the Japanese colonialism has left a deleterious impact on the Korean community that is self-defeating in mentality. Koreans often give a carte blanche for the victimizers to continue unchecked and unquestioned.

One can see the extent to which Japanese colonization has damaged the Korean community and the Korean psyche. As damaged as it is, the Korean psyche and will can be restored with active process and self-conscious will. And when the Korean-American community is brought to full health, it can do a lot to empower itself, advance itself, and benefit the society at large in the process.

The Korean-American experience in the United States is filled with heartaches. But along the way, many good Americans have shown their pro-active support. Korean-Americans can build on the positive forces and bravely fight the negative forces, whether they are self-defeatism, historical trauma, socio-political inaction, helping oppressors, or blaming the Korean victim. As Korean-Americans move forward proactively with self-awareness, it is certain that there are primarily positive elements in store for Korean-Americans as a community and as individuals.

The Great Korean Tragedy can be overcome!

About the Author

Christian Kim served as the president of the Cambridge University Korean Society (CUKS) in the United Kingdom during the 2002-2003 academic year. In the United States, Christian Kim served as the vice president of the Brown University Korean Graduate Students' Association in 1999. Christian Kim is very actively involved in Korean issues. Currently, Christian Kim participates actively in the Korean Oxbridge Theologians Association and Cambridge Korean Clergy Association in the United Kingdom.

http://www.TheHermitKingdomPress.com

www.ingramcontent.com/pod-product-compliance
Lightning Source LLC
Chambersburg PA
CBHW032302150426
43195CB00008BA/542